REJECTION
Healing a Wounded Heart

JUNE HUNT

AspirePress

Torrance, California

ROSE PUBLISHING/ASPIRE PRESS

CONTENTS

ear friend,

Years ago, I came to this excruciating conclusion: *Nothing* cuts to the core as deeply as rejection. Even death, while heartbreaking, doesn't leave such lasting wounds.

As a child, I longed for a family like the Andersons on *Father Knows Best*. How I wanted a dad who loved me, who would listen to me. My friends seemed to have daddies like that—ones who were interested in their activities, ones who were involved. When problems erupted in their families, they were eventually resolved with heart-to-heart talks. In contrast, my family life and my father were completely different.

I remember watching the happy "TV families" talking around their dinner tables, and then I would compare our family. Oh, we also gathered around the dinner table, but we children were told that we could speak only if we had something to say of interest to *everyone*. *Everyone* actually meant Dad. And nothing my siblings or I ever said or did was of interest to him. So we ate in silence, listening to Dad and his frequent guests pontificate about politics and world affairs. (Truthfully, Mother would have relished hearing us talk, but she believed her duty was to sit quietly and keep us from "disturbing the peace.")

With each passing year, I felt the sting of rejection even more. I spent several summers at a beautiful camp in Colorado, but I hated Colorado only because I had been "sent away." Numerous times Dad would sternly say, *"You are a bad influence on your mother."* I couldn't get past the fact that I'd been *sent away.*

The one time that I confronted my dad about the way he treated Mother, he responded violently—physically—toward me. And then, within two days, I was shipped off to boarding school. Again I hated it. Although the school had a reputation for "educational excellence," my grades dropped to a string of Ds and Fs. As a mere sophomore in high school, I walked from class to class with the raw wounds of rejection, never sharing with a soul the hurts hidden in my heart. Rejection and dejection were my closest companions.

Have you, too, walked the lonely road of rejection? If so, you know the silent cry for acceptance, that inner need for intimacy, your deep craving for closeness.

What an indescribable comfort to know that even when my "outer circumstances" had not changed I could experience true acceptance, intimacy, and closeness, and that in the midst of my pain there was One who would never, ever reject me. He is the One who has already suffered great rejection *for* me. His name is Jesus. With His presence in my life, He began the process of healing my wounded heart, from the inside out, and He can do the same for anyone who has been rejected.

If you too have experienced that severe pain of rejection, I'm so glad you've met me here. As you read these pages, you will learn the greatest story of rejection and redemption. And my prayer is that you will realize how God feels about you and discover the deepest security that only His love and acceptance can provide.

Yours in the Lord's hope,

June

June Hunt

"I have loved you with an everlasting love; I have drawn you with loving-kindness."
(Jeremiah 31:3)

REJECTION
Healing a Wounded Heart

Nothing can ravage your heart like rejection. The most penetrating wound is the painful rejection of a loved one. Even death itself does not pierce your heart as deeply as when you know you have been abandoned. You feel devastated when someone dear to your heart deserts you. Rejection chips away at your self-image. It chisels down your confidence and challenges your hope. Meanwhile, the memory of your loved one lingers on and on in the recesses of your mind, repeating—through whispers and shouts—those haunting messages: "You are unwelcome. You are unworthy."

Is your heart broken? Is your spirit crushed? Nothing is more healing than to know that the Lord loves you unconditionally. He accepts you eternally. When your pain seems endless and your heart is tender to the touch, continue to put yourself into His compassionate hands. He will hold you with His heart of love until there is true healing, for ...

"The Lord is close to the brokenhearted and saves those who are crushed in spirit." (Psalm 34:18)

DEFINITIONS

Favoritism can be extremely painful. Children catch on quickly when there is a "favorite" in the family. The favored child often comes late in life—late like young Joseph in the Bible, the beloved son of Jacob. In his heart, the father not only favors Joseph over his ten brothers, but also flaunts his favoritism by giving Joseph the infamous "coat of many colors"—a coat Jacob himself has made! Meanwhile, the older brothers seethe with anger at the sight of this richly ornamented robe, which has now become a symbol of their father's painful rejection. Little did Jacob know that his own favoritism would be the breeding ground for jealousy—the spark that would create a climate of hurt, hostility, and lasting hatred.

**"Now Israel [Jacob] loved Joseph more than any of his other sons, because he had been born to him in his old age; and he made a richly ornamented robe for him. When his brothers saw that their father loved him more than any of them, they hated him and could not speak a kind word to him."
(Genesis 37:3–4)**

Have you ever wondered, *What was the very first rejection on earth?* The first rejection is recorded in the first book of the Bible. God gives Adam and Eve everything they will ever need. He also gives one warning, "Don't eat *from that one tree.*" And what do they do? They eat *from that one tree!* Their direct defiance means that they reject not just God's Word, but also God Himself (Genesis 2:15–17; 3:6).

▶*Rejection* is the act of refusing to accept or consider a person or thing that is not wanted or not approved.[1]

- When you experience rejection, you feel unloved, unwanted, unacceptable.

- The Greek verb *apodokimazo* means "to reject as the result of examination and disapproval."[2] (*apo* = away from, *dokimazo* = to approve)

- Jesus felt the pain of rejection. The Bible refers to Christ as the "Cornerstone"—the vital, the most essential stone of a major structure—yet He was the cornerstone (or capstone) the builders rejected.

"The stone the builders rejected has become the capstone." (Matthew 21:42)

9

▶ ***To be rejected*** is to be cast aside, cast off, cast away—to be thrown away as having no value.[3]

- When you are rejected, you can feel useless, abandoned, worthless.

- The Greek verb *atheteo* means "to do away with, to set aside, to cast or throw away as useless or unsatisfactory."[4]

- Jesus challenged the Pharisees and teachers of the law because they were rejecting the laws of God.

"You have a fine way of setting aside the commands of God in order to observe your own traditions!" (Mark 7:9)

▶ ***To reject*** someone means to despise, refuse, shun, turn away from.[5]

- If you reject others, you use your attitudes and actions to reveal the condition of your heart.

- The Hebrew word *maas* means "to reject, refuse, despise."[6]

- Because God has given each of us free will, we may choose to reject the Word of God and even God Himself.

"The wise will be put to shame; they will be dismayed and trapped. Since they have rejected the word of the LORD, what kind of wisdom do they have?" (Jeremiah 8:9)

QUESTION: "My father died six years ago, but I'm still having trouble dealing with the anger I've had toward him. He was partial to my brother, but treated my sister, my mother, and me like second-class citizens. I tried to please him with my achievements, but we never communicated and he never recognized my accomplishments. How can I stop being so controlled by my anger?"

ANSWER: Anger has four sources: hurt, fear, frustration, and injustice. The anger you describe comes from at least three of the four. The rejection you experienced is very hurtful. Seeking to please him and never achieving recognition is extremely frustrating, and being treated in a negative way simply because you are a female is most unjust. The truth is that his treatment of you had nothing to do with you, but everything to do with him. He was the one in the wrong. His inadequacies let you down. Recognize this truth and turn loose of your expectations regarding him. Admit that your father was unable to be loving and accept him simply for being your father. Choose to forgive and release him to God so that your anger does not produce bitterness in your own heart. *"See to it that no one misses the grace of God and that no bitter root grows up to cause trouble and defile many"* (Hebrews 12:15).

Joseph understood rejection. Although he was his father's favorite son, Joseph was betrayed by his brothers. Imagine Joseph as a teenager—he suddenly finds himself jerked out of his comfortable home, only to be carted off to a foreign country to live as a stranger, to live as a slave! The grief of losing his family must have been frightening.

Still, Joseph accepted the will of God in his life, which enabled him to accept the sovereignty of God over his life. In spite of one betrayal after another, Joseph refused to become bitter. Instead, he accepted his circumstances by humbly entrusting himself to God.

As years passed, Joseph rose to a position of highest respect and power. When his brothers journeyed to Egypt in search of grain, they found themselves at the mercy of Joseph. Immediately, he knew who *they* were—but they didn't know who *he* was!

Did he take revenge and refuse to give them grain? Did he send them off *with grain*, but not acknowledge them as brothers? Did he extend his hand of help, but insist they bow before him?

No. Joseph refused resentment—he accepted

his brothers despite their past betrayal. By inviting them to become part of his life once again, they knew his acceptance was not merely *conditional*, but rather *unconditional*. And, in truth, his acceptance was possible only because of the condition of his heart—his heart of true forgiveness, which allowed him to focus on the future, and his heart of true commitment, which enabled him to let the past stay in the past. (Read Genesis 37:12–29 and chapters 41–45.)

▶ *To accept* someone means to approve or to receive that one favorably or willingly.[7] We should receive and value others because of their God-given worth.

- Your acceptance of others is based on the disposition of your heart, which, in turn, is expressed through your attitude and actions.

- The Greek word *proslambano* means "to accept, receive, welcome."[8]

- Jesus Christ provides the supreme example of acceptance. The Bible says we are to accept others the same way Christ accepts us.

**"Accept one another, then,
just as Christ accepted you,
in order to bring praise to God."
(Romans 15:7)**

When we reject someone, if we look closely, we may find that we are repeating the same rejection that we ourselves have received. The same is true of those who have learned to be accepting of others. Typically, we give what has been given to us. However, *your past rejection need not determine your future.* You can grow in your ability to become more and more accepting—even when you yourself have been rejected. The Bible says ...

> **"Forget the former things;**
> **do not dwell on the past."**
> **(Isaiah 43:18)**

The Three Levels of Acceptance[9]

1 Zero Acceptance

- "No matter what I do, I'll never be accepted."

The person who *totally rejects* you harbors deep hurt and bitterness and extends no grace and mercy. But the Bible says ...

"Get rid of all bitterness, rage and anger, brawling and slander, along with every form of malice. Be kind and compassionate to one another, forgiving each other,

just as in Christ God forgave you."
(Ephesians 4:31–32)

2 Performance-based Acceptance

- "I feel accepted only when I perform perfectly."

The person who accepts you based only on *how you act* demands, "You must meet my requirements," and rarely offers grace and mercy. But the Bible says ...

"Judgment without mercy will be shown to anyone who has not been merciful. Mercy triumphs over judgment!" (James 2:13)

3 Unconditional Acceptance

- "No matter what I do, even when I fail, I always feel accepted."

The person who accepts you—especially when you fail—lives with a heart of grace and mercy and reflects the heart of God. The Bible says ...

"Show mercy and compassion to one another." (Zechariah 7:9)

QUESTION: "Can an authentic Christian be rejected by God?"

ANSWER: No. Based on various verses in the Bible, an authentic Christian who has truly trusted in Christ will still sin but will never be rejected by God. If you find yourself fearful of being forsaken by God, claim the following truth from God's unchanging Word:

"For the LORD will not reject his people; he will never forsake his inheritance." (Psalm 94:14)

CHARACTERISTICS OF THOSE FEELING REJECTED[10]

The teenage years can be replete with life's most painful rejections. Because of severe insecurity, young people crave acceptance from others and often overreact to any rejection.

By age seventeen, Joseph felt the sting of rejection from his older brothers. But, in truth, Joseph played a part in causing his brothers' jealousy. Although God had given Joseph a special ability to interpret dreams, Joseph unwisely disclosed a certain dream to his older brothers which implied that one day they would all bow down to him. Speaking these words was not smart on Joseph's part!

> *"Joseph had a dream, and when he told it to his brothers, they hated him all the more. He said to them, 'Listen to this dream I had: We were binding sheaves of grain out in the field when suddenly my sheaf rose and stood upright, while your sheaves gathered around mine and bowed down to it.'"*
> (Genesis 37:5–7)

How insulting! How impertinent! How arrogant! Resenting the implication that Joseph would "lord" over them, his brothers continued to be filled with an animosity that eventually reached a boiling point. These brothers, who felt such intense rejection, in turn took revenge and made sure that Joseph would pay dearly. Joseph's brothers did not realize that although some say, "Revenge is sweet," it can also leave a bitter aftertaste. That is why the Bible says ...

**"See to it that ... no bitter root grows up to cause trouble and defile many."
(Hebrews 12:15)**

If your sense of self-worth is based on the approval of others, you are on a runaway roller coaster with no ability to control when you are up or down. Your feeling of value is at the mercy of what others think about you. Your sense of identity is determined by how others respond to you. To get off this uncontrollable roller coaster and conquer your fear of rejection, allow the Lord to control your life. He created you and established your worth when He made you in His image. As you put your trust in Him, He will turn your fear into faith because ...

**"Fear of man will prove to be a snare,
but whoever trusts
in the Lord is kept safe."
(Proverbs 29:25)**

Messages of One Who Is Addicted to the Approval of Others

If you think you may be living for the approval of others, honestly evaluate the following statements to see if they reflect your self-talk.

- "I am not good enough."
- "I have to try harder."
- "I have to earn your love."
- "I have to be perfect."
- "I can never please you."
- "I always feel stupid."
- "I am always the one at fault."
- "I am not acceptable in the eyes of others."
- "I know that what I think isn't important."
- "I know there is nothing likeable about me."
- "I don't deserve to be loved."
- "I don't feel anyone could really love me."
- "I don't feel that God could ever love me."

Even though you may think these thoughts are true about yourself, they don't reflect God's truth. The Bible says . . .

"This is love: not that we loved God, but that he loved us and sent his Son as an atoning sacrifice for our sins."
(1 John 4:10)

The Fear of Rejection Test[11]

If we feel controlled by the fear of rejection, then our focus will be on being "people pleasers." However, we need to say what the apostle Paul said:

"We are not trying to please men but God." (1 Thessalonians 2:4)

If you are uncertain whether or not you are living for the approval of others, answer the following questions honestly to see if you live with the fear of rejection.

▶ Do you avoid certain people out of fear that they will reject you?

▶ Do you become anxious when you think someone might not accept you?

▶ Do you feel awkward around others who are different from you?

▶ Do you feel disturbed when someone is not friendly toward you?

▶ Do you work hard at trying to determine what people think of you?

▶ Do you become depressed when others are critical of you?

▶ Do you consider yourself basically shy and unsociable around others?

▶ Do you try to see the negative in others?

▶ Do you find yourself trying to impress others?

▶ Do you repeat negative messages about yourself to yourself?

▶ Do you look for clues as to how others are responding to you in order to avoid the pain of rejection?

▶ Do you say "Yes" when you should say "No" to others?

▶ Do you expect others to respond to situations and conversations in the same way you would?

▶ Do you hear people saying that you are a "codependent person"?

▶ Do you experience hypersensitivity to the opinions of others but insensitivity to your own emotions?

▶ Do you often feel overly controlled by others?

▶ Do you struggle with anger and resentment toward others?

▶ Do you seem to be easily manipulated by others?

If you conclude that you have been controlled by the fear of rejection and you have lived for the approval of others, take this verse to heart:

"Am I now trying to win the approval of men, or of God? Or am I trying to please men? If I were still trying to please men, I would not be a servant of Christ."
(Galatians 1:10)

What are the ramifications of rejection? Perhaps you've been unaware of its subtle impact on your soul (your mind, will, and emotions). One obvious assault that rejection makes on your soul is an altering of your own self-perception and the inevitable insecurities that seem to arise out of nowhere when someone painfully turns away from you. That rejection can sear the deepest part of your soul and at the same time "mess with" your mind, taint your thoughts, and make you question your ability to function normally. But God, who knows every rejection you will ever encounter, never planned for you to be emotionally or spiritually *disabled*. Although you will be rejected, the Bible says ...

"God is able to make all grace abound to you, so that in all things at all times, having all that you need, you will abound in every good work."
(2 Corinthians 9:8)

The following are many of the classic symptoms of those who have been rejected in the past and as a result have a fear of future rejection.

▶ *Ambivalence*—"I have difficulty making decisions— if I make the wrong decision, I could be rejected."

▶ *Anxiety*—"I have real apprehension when someone says, 'Trust me.'"

▶ *Bitterness*—"I harbor bitterness toward those who rejected me and toward God, who allowed it to happen."

▶ *Depression*—"My heart feels so heavy. The pain has pushed me down."

▶ *Distrust*—"I can't really trust others not to desert me."

▶ *Escapism*—"Life hurts. I just need to numb the pain."

▶ *Fear*—"I live in fear of being rejected again."

▶ *Flat emotions*—"My heart is so deeply hurt that I can't seem to feel excited about anything."

▶ *Guilt/false guilt*—"I feel so bad about myself. No wonder I was rejected."

▶ *Inability to accept love*—"Even if others say that they love me, I know it's not true."

▶ *Inferiority*—"I know I'll never measure up!"

▶ *Insensitivity*—"I can't feel for others who are in pain."

▶ *Introspective*—"I've got to keep analyzing what's wrong with me."

▶ *Low self-worth*—"I know I'm not worthy of being accepted."

▶ *Resignation*—"Whatever will be, will be, so why try?"

▶ *Self-condemnation*—"I feel terrible. I know I'm to blame whenever I'm rejected."

▶ *Self-pity*—"I'm always ignored. No one reaches out to me."

▶ *Self-rejection*—"I wish I'd never been born!"

▶ *Withdrawal*—"I'm not willing to be vulnerable again."

▶ *Worry*—"I'm afraid I'll be scarred for life."

The unseen pain of rejection can sabotage your soul and shatter your spirit; however, the outer signs of rejection are easily seen and even felt by others. When someone special walks out of your life, the joy of living is snuffed out like having a wet towel thrown on a lit candle. The darkness of desertion can discolor your perception of others and do untold damage to your relationships. The saddest part of it all is that rejection breeds *rejection*!

In truth, no one can avoid being rejected or treated unjustly at times. However, when you remember that your identity is in the Lord, because of your relationship with Him—not in your having been rejected by others—you will experience the truth that you, like Paul, can be ...

**" ... hard pressed on every side, but not crushed; perplexed, but not in despair; persecuted, but not abandoned; struck down, but not destroyed."
(2 Corinthians 4:8–9)**

Many of the outer signs of rejection are:

▶ *Abuse*—Mistreating others and even yourself

▶ *Addiction*—Seeking solace in addictive behavior in an effort to numb your pain.

▶ *Anger*—Feeling bitterness toward others and even toward God

▶ *Apathy*—Giving up on life—not caring about anything

▶ *Arrogance*—Acting superior to others

▶ *Competitive*—Assuming, I have to be the best

▶ *Critical spirit*—Being condescending toward others

▶ *Defensive*—Arguing with others for self-protection

▶ *Dominant*—Controlling others and situations to an excess

▶ *Exaggeration*—Bragging to impress others

▶ *Hatred*—Loathing (primarily directed toward yourself)

▶ *Isolation*—Becoming a loner as a means of self-protection

▶ *Jealousy*—Resenting suggestions and successes of others

▶ *Legalism*—Complying with rigid rules based on black-and-white thinking

▶ *People pleasing*—Trying too hard to please others

▶ *Perfectionism*—Feeling like a failure unless you do everything perfectly

▶ *Performance-based acceptance*—Believing your acceptance is based only on how well you perform

▶ *Rebellion*—Resisting the authority of others

▶ *Subservient*—Cowering in the presence of others

▶ *Undisciplined*—Lacking self-control and boundaries around others

▶ *Vengeful*—Getting even with others

When you experienced painful rejection in the past, do you remember rehearsing repeated thoughts, feelings, and perhaps even "vows"? Unfortunately, these repetitious thoughts (*I'm not accepted*) and emotions (*I feel unwanted*) lead to an illogical conclusion (*I vow that no one will hurt me again*).

How we live our lives is based on what we *believe*. Therefore, *if we believe we are rejected, we will live a life of rejection* in our minds, our hearts, and our emotions, *even when we are not outwardly rejected by others*.

▶ Repeated Thoughts:

- "No one loves me."
- "No one cares about me."
- "I don't really matter."
- "I'm not good enough."
- "I don't fit in."
- "I'm not accepted."

▶ Repeated Feelings:

- "I feel empty inside."
- "I feel all alone."
- "I feel insignificant."

- "I feel like I'm not worth anything."
- "I feel unwanted."
- "I feel excluded."

▶ Repeated Vows:

- "I'm not going to get close to anyone again."
- "I'm not going to let anyone be important to me again."
- "No one will ever hurt me again."

This progression demonstrates the importance of taking your thoughts captive, training your mind, telling yourself the truth. You are accepted by God; therefore, allow Him to heal your heart from the pain of the past. If you will cancel the vows that are contrary to God's Word, you will experience perfect peace in your life.

**"We demolish arguments
and every pretension that sets itself up
against the knowledge of God,
and we take captive every thought to
make it obedient to Christ."
(2 Corinthians 10:5)**

Individuals from a childhood of rejection often have immense difficulty trusting God because of "projection"—they project onto God the negative characteristics of their authority figures. If their earthly fathers rejected them, they perceive the heavenly Father to be rejecting them. If they had an untrustworthy mother, then God must be untrustworthy. These negative perceptions make learning the true character of God essential and sometimes very difficult.

"The LORD is a refuge for the oppressed, a stronghold in times of trouble. Those who know your name will trust in you, for you, LORD, have never forsaken those who seek you." (Psalm 9:9–10)

Reactions against God[15]

Sometimes those who have been rejected:

▶ **Resent** God for allowing the rejection

▶ **Regard** God as a tyrannical judge and jury

▶ **Reflect** the negative attributes of childhood authority figures onto God

▶ **Rely** on self-protection and deny the protection of God

▶ **Refuse** to accept the authority of God

▶ **Rebel** against the Word of God

▶ **Reject** statements about the love of God

▶ **Resist** the thought of trusting God

▶ **Recoil** from true fellowship with God

▶ **React** to their fear of condemnation from God instead of embracing the love of God

Regardless of the rejection from your past authority figures, the Bible gives this powerful promise:

**"Be strong and courageous.
Do not be afraid or terrified
because of them, for the LORD your God
goes with you; he will never leave you
nor forsake you."
(Deuteronomy 31:6)**

CAUSES OF REJECTION

People reject other people for different reasons. We are rejected at times because of *something we have done* or *something someone else has done.* At other times, the rejection is not based on what we have done but merely on who we are and, therefore, on *something or someone we represent.* In Joseph's case, he felt the boiling rejection of his brothers for all three reasons.

▶ First: What He Did

The brothers knew Joseph had tattled on them to their father (Genesis 37:2). That certainly did not win Joseph any favor in their eyes! He really added fuel to the fire when he told them about his two dreams of how he would one day be in a position of authority over them (Genesis 37:5–7, 9).

▶ Second: What His Father Did

They envied Joseph because of the coat his father made for him (Genesis 37:3).

▶ Third: Who He Was

They resented Joseph because of who he was. He was the son of Rachel, their father's favorite wife—their father's beloved wife—

and thus Joseph was his father's favorite child.

In reality, Joseph was more of a *prophet* than a *politician* or he certainly would not have spoken of those dreams with his brothers, who already despised him. Although Jacob rebuked Joseph for *the way* he spoke, Jacob also kept what Joseph said in mind.

**"When he told his father as well as his brothers, his father rebuked him and said, 'What is this dream you had? Will your mother and I and your brothers actually come and bow down to the ground before you?' His brothers were jealous of him, but his father kept the matter in mind."
(Genesis 37:10–11)**

Some of the reasons people feel rejected are obvious. Think about a difficult time when you felt devalued; you felt dejected and deserted. Was the reason for your piercing pain obvious? Often, the loneliest times of your life can be readily understood because you were *overtly* rejected. Your feelings are sometimes a result of having been rejected. But the wonderful Word of God tells us that while others may cast us away, we can cast ourselves upon the Lord.

> **"From birth I was cast upon you;
> from my mother's womb
> you have been my God."
> (Psalm 22:10)**

▶ *Abandonment*—Feeling *forsaken* because someone special is no longer there for you.

▶ *Adoption*—Feeling *unloved* because your focus is on having been "given away" (instead of on feeling loved because you were "placed in a loving home").

▶ *Cast away*—Feeling *worthless* because you were "in the way" and therefore you have been thrown out of the home or sent away (to camp, to boarding school, to other relatives).

▶ *Childhood sexual abuse*—Feeling *shamed* because your sexual boundaries were violated by abusers inside or outside your family.

▶ *Disapproval*—Feeling *flawed* because you can't measure up to what is expected: "I know I'll never be good enough for you."

▶ *Divorce*—Feeling *deserted* because your parents split up or because you and your spouse divorced. (Some parents feel deserted by their own children.)

▶ *Domestic violence*—Feeling *degraded* because of physical attacks from one of your family members.

▶ *Excessive punishment*—Feeling *devalued* because your parents were excessively harsh.

▶ *Favoritism*—Feeling *disregarded* because someone else is preferred over you.

▶ *Greed*—Feeling *discredited* because someone takes credit for your ideas or work or because someone steals your money or possessions.

▶ *Hostility*—Feeling *alienated* because of constant fighting and name-calling.

▶ *Humiliation*—Feeling *ridiculed* because your self-worth is being attacked.

▶ ***Indifference***—Feeling *discounted* because your existence is not acknowledged.

▶ ***Infidelity***—Feeling *betrayed* because your bond of trust has been breeched.

▶ ***Jilted***—Feeling *spurned* because of rejection in courtship, friendship, or marriage.

▶ ***Prejudice***—Feeling *ostracized* because of merely being "different."

▶ ***Rape***—Feeling *violated* because of date rape, mate rape, or stranger rape.

▶ ***Verbal Abuse***—Feeling *angry* because you don't know what you did to deserve such unjust treatment.

Just as there are obvious *overt* reasons for people to feel rejected, there are also not-so-obvious *covert* reasons. These covert causes are not easily identifiable because sometimes they are shrouded in secrecy. At other times they are sins of *omission* rather than *commission*. Whatever the reason, covert rejection cuts just as deeply as overt, if not deeper. Because these tactics go undetected, and therefore unchallenged, victims are left even more devastated. However, since God sees everything, nothing escapes His eye—especially those things concerning each of us, whom He carefully crafted.

"From heaven the Lord looks down and sees all mankind; from his dwelling place he watches all who live on earth—he who forms the hearts of all, who considers everything they do." (Psalm 33:13–15)

▶ *Absence of nurturing*

- Feeling *neglected* because of a lack of attention or affection. "There's a hole in my heart because I didn't feel loved."

▶ *Addictions*

- Feeling *ignored* because of an addiction (examples: alcohol/drugs, compulsive spending, inappropriate sexual behavior, gambling). The addiction is prioritized above the relationship. "Despite what you say, I know that (the addiction) is more important to you than I am."

▶ *Broken promises*

- Feeling *unimportant* because of a continual lack of commitment. "I'm not worth anything to you—you keep your word to others but not to me."

▶ *Comparison*

- Feeling *inferior* because of always being measured against others. "I have no intrinsic value."

▶ *Cliques*

- Feeling *unworthy* because of being excluded from a group. "I am not good enough to be accepted."

▶ *Critical spirit*

- Feeling *emotionally battered* because of the relentless judgmental attitudes of others. "I can never measure up to your standards."

▶ Death/critical illness

- Feeling *forgotten* because of being left alone (especially in the case of suicide). "Why did you have to leave me?"

▶ Discounted emotions

- Feeling *pushed aside* because what comes from your heart is dismissed. "What I feel isn't important to you."

▶ Gender discrimination

- Feeling *inferior* because of a bias against your gender—your gender is the wrong gender! "Nothing I think, say, or do has any validity to you because of your negative mindset toward me."

▶ Handicaps

- Feeling *inadequate* because of your limitations. "I am defective and not equal to others because I cannot do all that they can do."

▶ Lack of support

- Feeling *rebuffed* because of not being believed or helped. "You didn't support me when I desperately needed you."

▶ Loss of a pet

- Feeling *abandoned* because your pet

was the only one who accepted you unconditionally. "I just lost my best friend."

▶ *Overcontrolling*

- Feeling *powerless* because your individuality is denied. "You won't allow me to be myself."

▶ *Overindulgence*

- Feeling *helpless* because everything is done for you as though you cannot do anything for yourself. "I feel as though I'm being treated like a child."

▶ *Performance-based acceptance*

- Feeling *unacceptable* because you are valued only for what you do. "I'm accepted only if I perform to your expectation."

▶ *Sarcasm*

- Feeling *cut down* because of caustic humor at your expense. "Your sharp words, though masked with humor, feel like a sword piercing my heart."

▶ *Silent treatment*

- Feeling *shunned* because a loved one has intentionally stopped communicating with you. "You treat me as if I don't exist."

QUESTION: "My mother doesn't care about me or my problems. She doesn't spend time with me, and she doesn't show me any love or affection. Why does she continue to reject me?"

ANSWER: Sadly, many parents do not know how to nurture their children. Your mother's lack of love reveals that she is not emotionally whole—her rejection sheds a spotlight on the *hole in her heart.*

▶ Ask the Lord to help you stop taking her behavior personally. Her lack of love has *nothing to do with you.*

▶ Realize that the void within her heart restricts her from reaching out to your heart.

▶ Fully receive and focus on God's unconditional love for you. Although you have no power to make your mother express love, God will give you all the love and acceptance you need, empowering you to overcome the pain of rejection.

The Bible gives you this special assurance:

"Though my father and mother forsake me, the Lord will receive me."
(Psalm 27:10)

Our core beliefs control every area of our lives. Even when we don't *consciously* recognize their influence, they are still at work, silently penetrating our thoughts, feelings, and, inevitably, our actions. Identifying and changing our negative core beliefs will help us replace unhealthy, destructive actions with new behaviors that honor God and others. The Bible says ...

> **"Whatever you do,
> do it all for the glory of God."
> (1 Corinthians 10:31)**

Progression of Rejection[18]

Negative Core Belief

- "I have to have the approval of others."

Negative Thoughts

- "I'm not loved."
- "I am not significant."
- "I'm not accepted."

Negative Feeling

- "I feel rejected!"

Negative Actions

- Rejecting others

- Bitterness toward others
- Judging others
- Withdrawing from others

"Let us stop passing judgment on one another." (Romans 14:13)

Replace the Old Progression with the New[19]

New Core Belief

- "I won't always have the approval of everyone, but I have the approval of God."

New Thoughts

- "I'm unconditionally loved by God."
- "I am significant to God."
- "I am unconditionally accepted by God."

New Feeling

- "I feel accepted!"

New Actions

- Accepting others
- Forgiving others
- Seeing good in others
- Reaching out to others

"Let us consider how we may spur one another on toward love and good deeds." (Hebrews 10:24)

QUESTION: "How can I overcome the extreme fear of rejection that I've struggled with for a long time? I have so much fear that I've become isolated from people."

ANSWER: God does not want you to be controlled by fear, but instead to be controlled by Christ, who will enable you to overcome your fear. Therefore, the first step in gaining victory over your fear of rejection is to give control of your life to the Lord Jesus Christ. Rely on His strength within you to face every rejection in your life. As you look back at your past, write down every remembrance of rejection from the first instance until the present.

▶ Take time to feel the pain of each experience and then put into writing how you felt.

▶ Go back to the beginning, slowly reading through your list and with each situation say, "That was then and this is now. I will not let the pain of my past control my future."

▶ Release each painful rejection to the Lord. "Lord Jesus, I release my fear of this pain into your hands."

▶ Begin talking with one, wise person whom you think you can trust. (Tell this person what you are trying to overcome and ask if he or she would be willing to help you.)

▶Do not focus on what you think others are thinking about you, but instead trust in God's unconditional acceptance of you.

"Fear of man will prove to be a snare, but whoever trusts in the LORD is kept safe." (Proverbs 29:25)

WHAT IS the Root Cause of Rejection?

All of us are created with three God-given inner needs—the need for love, for significance, and for security.[20] We experience rejection from our earliest years when we are deprived of having someone who loves us unconditionally, someone who regards us as highly significant, or someone who welcomes us as part of "a family." (Your parents may have divorced, your feelings may have been snubbed, or your loved one may have left.) Since people do fail people, it is essential not to let other people define who you are. Realize that rejection can quickly skew your view! Even though you may not see the path you should take, the Lord promises to guide all your steps and meet all your needs.

"The LORD will guide you always; he will satisfy your needs in a sun-scorched land and will strengthen your frame. You will be like a well-watered garden, like a spring whose waters never fail."
(Isaiah 58:11)

▶ **WRONG BELIEF:**

"Because of being rejected, I feel so unloved, so insignificant, so unwanted. My life isn't worth anything!"

▶ **RIGHT BELIEF:**

"I do not like being rejected, but I know my worth isn't based on whether or not others reject me but on the fact that the Lord accepts me. Jesus not only loved me enough to die for my sins, but He also lives inside me and will never leave me nor forsake me."

"I trust in your unfailing love;
my heart rejoices in your salvation."
(Psalm 13:5)

QUESTION: "Even though I am a Christian, I feel like God rejects me. Others have also rejected me. What can I do about the self-condemnation I feel and the bitterness that is just eating me up inside?"

ANSWER: Bitterness is the result of unresolved, prolonged anger. Self-condemnation is anger turned inward. This means that before you can deal with bitterness or self-condemnation, you need to look into your past and uncover the root of your feelings.

Start by determining the cause of your anger. Remember, anger has four sources—hurt, injustice, fear, and frustration. Did something in your past make you feel one of these painful emotions? Then realize that feelings almost always follow thinking; in other words, once you have discovered the source of your anger, check out the truthfulness of your thinking—only the truth can set you free. Once you've established the truth, renew your mind by repeating that truth. First and foremost, repeat Romans 8:1 and pray, "Thank you, God, that because of Christ you will never condemn or reject me." The next time you feel rejected, remember that *"Christ in you, the hope of glory"* (Colossians 1:27) can enable you to overcome your fear and know your true acceptance in God's eyes. "There is now no condemnation for those who are in Christ Jesus" (Romans 8:1).

STEPS TO SOLUTION

The strongest lesson to glean from Joseph's life is his *response to repeated rejection*. (See Genesis chapters 37–50.) His father, Jacob, sends Joseph to the fields to find his brothers, but upon seeing him, the brothers conspire to kill him. Instead, they sell him to merchants who cart him off to Egypt and sell him as a slave to prominent Potiphar. In spite of this severe rejection, Joseph never becomes bitter or blames God. He faithfully performs whatever work is given to him with excellence and integrity. Yet the day comes when the wife of his master tries to seduce Joseph. Although he resists, Joseph is falsely accused and imprisoned. At any time during Joseph's years in exile, he could have allowed hatred to fill his heart, but he didn't.

Twenty-two years later, famine reaches his boyhood homeland, and his family becomes desperate. So his father sends his sons to Egypt to purchase food. Little do they know that the brother whom they had rejected has now become prime minister of Egypt. What an opportunity for Joseph to banish his brothers from the land! But rather than returning rejection for rejection, Joseph weeps and reveals his true identity. Rather than taking revenge, he accepts his brothers and extends his heart of forgiveness and his hand of help. Even his words are framed in unmistakable mercy when he says ...

"You intended to harm me, but God intended it for good to accomplish what is now being done, the saving of many lives." (Genesis 50:20)

KEY VERSE TO MEMORIZE

"The LORD himself goes before you and will be with you; he will never leave you nor forsake you. Do not be afraid; do not be discouraged."
(Deuteronomy 31:8)

Key Passage to Read and Reread

We know we will be rejected by the world because Jesus was rejected by the world. Sometimes "the world" is within our own families, just as it was within His own family. This means we may be rejected by *our own*, just as Jesus was rejected by *His own*. Decide now not to be dismayed or destroyed by rejection, but rather expect it and be strengthened by it. Remember, the heavier the burden, the stronger His strength to help you bear it.

**"Praise be to the Lord,
to God our Savior,
who daily bears our burdens."
(Psalm 68:19)**

Romans 8:28–39

In spite of my rejection ...

▶ God will work everything together for my good. (v. 28)

▶ God has called me to live according to His purpose. (v. 28)

▶ God has predetermined to conform me to Christ's character. (v. 29)

▶ God called me, justified me, and will glorify me. (v. 30)

▶ God is for me—no one can prevail against me. (v. 31)

▶ God did not spare His own Son, but gave Him up for me. (v. 32)

▶ God will, out of His grace, give me everything I need. (v. 32)

▶ God chose me; therefore, no one can condemn me. (v. 33)

▶ God Himself has vindicated me. (v. 33)

▶ God raised Christ from death to life; therefore, no one can condemn me. (v. 34)

▶ God placed Christ at His right hand to intercede for me. (v. 34)

▶ God's plan is that nothing can separate me from Christ's love. (v. 35)

▶ God's love compels me to face death willingly. (v. 36)

▶ God has made me more than a conqueror through Christ, who loves me. (v. 37)

▶ God's love has convinced me that nothing in my life or death

- neither angels nor demons,

- neither the present nor the future,

- nor any powers or principalities,

- neither height nor depth,

- nor anything else in all creation can separate me from the love of God. (vv. 38–39)

"I am convinced that neither death nor life, neither angels nor demons, neither the present nor the future, nor any powers, neither height nor depth, nor anything else in all creation, will be able to separate us from the love of God that is in Christ Jesus our Lord."
(Romans 8:38–39)

Did you grow up in a home where you never measured up, where you were mistreated, where you were maligned, and as a result, you're convinced God could never approve of you? Have you committed some hidden sin or harbored hatred in your heart and now you feel beyond the reach of God's forgiveness? Were you told, "You should *never* have been born. You were *never* wanted. You will *never* amount to anything"? If you are thoroughly persuaded that God has rejected you, then you don't know the God of the Bible and His special plan for you. The Lord says ...

"For I know the plans I have for you ...
plans to prosper you and not
to harm you, plans to give you
hope and a future."
(Jeremiah 29:11)

What Do You Need to Know about God?

▶ **Know God's character:**

- God is love.

  "God is love." (1 John 4:8)

- God loves you.

  "I have loved you with an everlasting love; I have drawn you with loving-kindness." (Jeremiah 31:3)

▶ **Know God's heart:**

- God wants to adopt you into His family.

  "How great is the love the Father has lavished on us, that we should be called children of God!" (1 John 3:1)

- God wants to be your guide through life.

  "Trust in the Lord with all your heart and lean not on your own understanding; in all your ways acknowledge him, and he will make your paths straight." (Proverbs 3:5–6)

▶ **Know God's plan:**

- God offers salvation to all.

  "God did not send his Son into the world to condemn the world, but to save the world through him." (John 3:17)

- God wants everyone to be saved, including you.

"He is patient with you, not wanting anyone to perish, but everyone to come to repentance." (2 Peter 3:9)

▶ **Know God's purposes:**

- God uses rejection to produce hope and Christlikeness.

"We also rejoice in our sufferings, because we know that suffering produces perseverance; perseverance, character; and character, hope. And hope does not disappoint us." (Romans 5:3–5)

- God gives you compassion and comfort, which, in turn, you can give to others.

"The Father of compassion and the God of all comfort ... comforts us in all our troubles, so that we can comfort those in any trouble with the comfort we ourselves have received from God. For just as the sufferings of Christ flow over into our lives, so also through Christ our comfort overflows." (2 Corinthians 1:3–5)

What Is the Key to God's Acceptance?

Have you ever tried to open a door with a key—but it was the wrong key? It won't work! Unless you use the *right key,* you cannot get inside. God has already shared the "Key" to entering into an everlasting relationship with Him, the Key to never being rejected.

FOUR POINTS YOU NEED TO KNOW

1 You have entered through the wrong door—*You (like everyone else) have chosen to sin.*

You cannot find your way to acceptance with God if you have entered through the wrong door. The Bible says that we all have sinned—not one of us is perfect. Each time we willfully choose to go our own way, not God's way, we sin.

"All have sinned and fall short of the glory of God." (Romans 3:23)

2 You have lost the key to God's acceptance—*Your sin separates you from God.*

You cannot open a locked door without the right key. Your own sin has locked the right door, the door to God, and you have no key to open that door. Because God's character is morally perfect (He is without sin), our sin results in a "penalty" or consequence. The Bible says that the consequence of our sin is separation from God. Actually, by choosing your own way, you have separated yourself from God.

"Your iniquities [sins] have separated you from your God." (Isaiah 59:2)

3 **You have been given a new Key to God's door of acceptance—***God provided the way for you to be forgiven.*

The heavenly Father sent His own Son, Jesus, to die on the cross to pay the penalty for your sins. You deserved to die, but instead, Christ died for you. God offers to you the only Key—the Lord Jesus Christ—that will open the door to God's eternal acceptance.

"God demonstrates his own love for us in this: While we were still sinners, Christ died for us." (Romans 5:8)

4 **You can open the door of acceptance—***You can receive God's forgiveness and peace by trusting in Jesus Christ now.*

While you may hold the Key to the door, you still have to unlock the door. You need to acknowledge that Jesus Christ died as your substitute, rely on what He did for you, and *ask Him to come into your life to take control of your life.* If you allow Him to be your Lord and Savior, He forgives you of your sins. And when you are forgiven, not only are you saved from separation from God, but you also are given the peace of God. He is standing at the door of your heart right now.

"Here I am! I stand at the door and knock. If anyone hears my voice and opens the door, I will come in and eat with him, and he with me." (Revelation 3:20)

If you desire to be fully forgiven by God—and to receive the peace of God—you can ask Jesus Christ to come into your life right now and give you His peace.

PRAYER OF SALVATION

"God, I want a secure relationship with You. I admit that many times I've rejected Your way and gone my way. Please forgive me for my sins. Jesus, thank You for dying on the cross for my sins. Come into my life to be my Lord and my Savior. Thank You for wanting me. Thank You for accepting me into Your family. Thank You that You will never leave me nor forsake me. In Your holy name I pray. Amen."

What Can You Expect Now?

If you sincerely prayed this prayer, listen to what God says!

"Since we have been justified [vindicated—declared righteous] through faith, we have peace with God through our Lord Jesus Christ." (Romans 5:1)

Without walking through the door to God's acceptance in response to His grace, people may sense God's rejection. Those who have been rejected, or who feel as if they have been, may enter into a cycle that leads to more rejection—a chain reaction, of sorts.

When you are rejected, a chain reaction can occur that leads to more rejection. Through a series of conscious choices, a cycle becomes a pattern that eventually becomes a way of life. When you are rejected, unless the truth is embraced (the cycle broken and the pattern replaced), the by-product of rejection will always be rejection.

Rejection Breeds Rejection

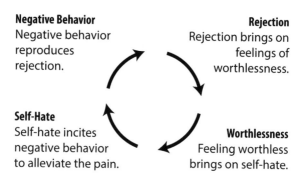

Negative Behavior
Negative behavior reproduces rejection.

Rejection
Rejection brings on feelings of worthlessness.

Self-Hate
Self-hate incites negative behavior to alleviate the pain.

Worthlessness
Feeling worthless brings on self-hate.

How Can You Break the Rejection Cycle?

Meditate on these statements and memorize these Scriptures.

▶**Rejection**

- "Just because someone rejects me doesn't mean that everyone rejects me. Jesus loves me, no matter what others choose to do."

  "As the Father has loved me, so have I loved you." (John 15:9)

- "Just because someone withholds love from me doesn't mean everyone will withhold love from me. God will always listen to me and will never withhold His love from me."

  "Praise be to God, who has not rejected my prayer or withheld his love from me!" (Psalm 66:20)

▶**Worthlessness**

- "Just because someone may think that I am worthless doesn't mean everyone thinks I'm worthless. God has already established my worth, and because of Him I will always have worth."

  "Are not five sparrows sold for two pennies? Yet not one of them is forgotten by God.

Indeed, the very hairs of your head are all numbered. Don't be afraid; you are worth more than many sparrows." (Luke 12:6–7)

- "Just because someone doesn't value me doesn't mean that no one values me. God values me enough to send Jesus to die for me so that I can spend eternity with Him!"

"For God so loved the world that he gave his one and only Son, that whoever believes in him shall not perish but have eternal life." (John 3:16)

▶ Self-hate

- "Just because someone has rejected me doesn't mean I should hate myself. God has always loved me, and I can rely on His love."

"We know and rely on the love God has for us. God is love." (1 John 4:16)

- "Just because someone has rejected me doesn't mean I should condemn myself. God will never condemn me, because I am in Christ's family."

"There is now no condemnation for those who are in Christ Jesus." (Romans 8:1)

▶ Negative behavior

- "Just because someone has rejected me doesn't mean I should act destructively by behaving in a way that sets me up for more rejection. Since I will pay for my bad choices and be rewarded for my good choices, I am going to make good choices."

"Do not be deceived: God cannot be mocked. A man reaps what he sows. The one who sows to please his sinful nature, from that nature will reap destruction; the one who sows to please the Spirit, from the Spirit will reap eternal life." (Galatians 6:7–8)

- "Just because someone has rejected me doesn't give me license to do what is wrong. God has given me the power to do what is right. Sin will not be my master!"

"If you do what is right, will you not be accepted? But if you do not do what is right, sin is crouching at your door; it desires to have you, but you must master it." (Genesis 4:7)

QUESTION: "Ever since my closest friend rejected me, I expect other friends to do the same. How can I keep from feeling like a reject?"

ANSWER: When someone close to you rejects you, be aware of a tendency to "over-generalize"—assuming that others will reject you too. Fearing the worst, you inadvertently begin pushing your remaining friends away in order to prevent further hurt. When they respond negatively, you interpret their reaction as confirmation of your deepest fears. This vicious cycle can lead to a self-fulfilling prophecy and helps explain the saying, "Rejection breeds rejection." To stop feeling like a reject ...

▶Don't assume that one person's opinion reflects everyone's opinion.

▶Don't let one person's negative attitude toward you define you.

▶Realize that because Jesus is always faithful, when He calls you "friend," you can trust that His love will be with you always.

▶Nurture several friendships, focusing on God's description of how *true* friends treat one another—a true friend will never reject you. *"A friend loves at all times"* (Proverbs 17:17).

YOU ARE Accepted Even When Rejected[22]

How can you have faith that you are accepted when, at times, you *feel* rejected?

Basing faith on *feelings* is disastrous for us all. *Feelings change, but God never does.* When we exercise *faith in what God has said* (based on our faithful God and His faithful Word), our minds and hearts will be renewed. Begin *telling yourself the truth* about your complete acceptance in Christ. During those times when you *feel* rejected by a special person, know that God has promised to walk into the darkness of your healing journey and shed light on your path. Despite the pain of past rejection, keep looking at the light of God's promise *never* to leave you nor forsake you.

"I will turn the darkness into light before them and make the rough places smooth. These are the things I will do; I will not forsake them."
(Isaiah 42:16)

Focus on Facts, Not Feelings

ADMIT THE REJECTION OF THE PAST AND ACKNOWLEDGE ITS PAIN.

▶ Ask God to bring to mind every rejection from your childhood to the present, and then consider the circumstances of each situation.

▶ Acknowledge the gamut of feelings of rejection you experienced with each past event. Release the pain and the person(s) involved to God.

▶ Ask God to heal the physical, emotional, and spiritual damage of each of these painful experiences of rejection.

"I remember my affliction and my wandering, the bitterness and the gall. I well remember them, and my soul is downcast within me. Yet this I call to mind and therefore I have hope: Because of the Lord's great love we are not consumed, for his compassions never fail. They are new every morning; great is your faithfulness." (Lamentations 3:19–23)

CLAIM GOD'S ACCEPTANCE AND UNCONDITIONAL LOVE.

▶ Confess God's love for you and the various ways He has shown you His love (for example, Christ's death for you).

▶ Cite Psalm 139:1–18 and praise God for orchestrating your conception, forming you in your mother's womb, and planning each day of your life.

▶ Convey your appreciation to God for His love of you by loving Him with all your heart, soul, mind, and strength. And love others as He loves you.

"'Though the mountains be shaken and the hills be removed, yet my unfailing love for you will not be shaken nor my covenant of peace be removed,' says the Lord, who has compassion on you." (Isaiah 54:10)

CHOOSE TO FORGIVE THOSE WHO REJECTED YOU.

▶ Consider all the hurt and anger you feel over your painful rejection.

▶ Count the cost of withholding forgiveness: a bitter spirit building up inside you, which will cause trouble and spread to those around you.

▶Commit to forgiving those who rejected you just as Christ forgave those who rejected Him (including you). Write down their names, their offenses, and the pain these individuals caused you. Then release each person, offense, and pain to God.

"Bear with each other and forgive whatever grievances you may have against one another. Forgive as the Lord forgave you." (Colossians 3:13)

EXPECT FUTURE REJECTION AS NATURAL IN A FALLEN WORLD.

▶Empty yourself of the pride that drives your desire to be accepted by everyone. Realize that it is *impossible* for you to gain everyone's approval, and then commit to pleasing God.

▶Empathize with others who feel rejected by friends, family, employers, business associates, or anyone else important to them.

▶Embrace, if you are a believer, the truth that according to the Bible, sharing in the sufferings of Christ is a privilege. As a believer you *will* experience rejection, just as Jesus did as a man. You are not exempt from being rejected in daily life. Jesus is rejected daily by those who refuse to turn to Him for salvation.

"Dear friends, do not be surprised at the painful trial you are suffering, as though something strange were happening to you. But rejoice that you participate in the sufferings of Christ, so that you may be overjoyed when his glory is revealed. If you are insulted because of the name of Christ, you are blessed, for the Spirit of glory and of God rests on you." (1 Peter 4:12–14)

PLANT SCRIPTURE IN YOUR MIND TO PRODUCE NEW THOUGHT PATTERNS.

▶ Purpose to renew your mind by selecting meaningful Scriptures to read, meditate on, and commit to memory. These will help you deal with any past, present, or possible future rejection.

▶ Plan a specific time each day to read God's Word and to pray.

▶ Partner with someone who will hold you accountable for applying God's truth to your heart.

"Do not conform any longer to the pattern of this world, but be transformed by the renewing of your mind. Then you will be able to test and approve what God's will

is—his good, pleasing and perfect will."
(Romans 12:2)

THANK GOD FOR WHAT YOU'VE LEARNED THROUGH YOUR REJECTION.

▶ "Thank you, Lord, for using my pain to make me more dependent on You."

▶ "Thank you, Lord, for using my pain to make me less dependent on people."

▶ "Thank you, Lord, for using my pain to make me more dependent on Your Word."

"It was good for me to be afflicted so that I might learn your decrees." (Psalm 119:71)

ENCOURAGE OTHERS AS AN EXPRESSION OF CHRIST'S LOVE.

▶ Extend compassion to those who are hurting as someone who has also been hurt.

▶ Enfold them in prayer—faithfully praying for them and with them.

▶ Ease emotional wounds by embracing those in pain and encouraging them to talk.

"Encourage one another daily."
(Hebrews 3:13)

Draw on the power of Christ's life within you.

▶ "I will see Christ as my security whenever I feel insecure."

▶ "I know that I have all I need, for Jesus will meet all my needs.

▶ "I will daily set aside my own selfish desires in favor of His desires, saying, 'Not my will, but Yours, Lord.'"

"I can do everything through him who gives me strength." (Philippians 4:13)

QUESTION: "Although I think I've been victorious over my fear of rejection, at times I've been overcome by a need to cling too strongly to others. Is there anything that will help refocus my mind when rejection begins to rule my heart?"

ANSWER: You *can* overcome the pain of any and all past rejection. The key to being an "overcomer" is to refocus—move your attention from the rejection to the fact that the Lord loves and accepts you. The way to change your focus is to repeat the truth over and over again.

"I will be glad and rejoice in your love, for you saw my affliction and knew the anguish of my soul." (Psalm 31:7)

When you are tempted to feel defeated, say to the Lord ...

▶ "Thank You, Lord, that You love me."

"This is how we know what love is: Jesus Christ laid down his life for us." (1 John 3:16)

▶ "Thank You, Lord, that You are with me."

"The LORD your God is with you, he is mighty to save. He will take great delight in you, he will quiet you with his love, he will rejoice over you with singing." (Zephaniah 3:17)

▶ "Thank You, Lord, that You forgive me."

"I acknowledged my sin to you and did not cover up my iniquity. I said, 'I will confess my transgressions to the LORD'— and you forgave the guilt of my sin." (Psalm 32:5)

▶ "Thank You, Lord, that You adopted me."

"To all who received him, to those who believed in his name, he gave the right to become children of God." (John 1:12)

▶ "Thank You, Lord, that You will complete the work You have begun in my life."

"He who began a good work in you will carry it on to completion until the day of Christ Jesus." (Philippians 1:6)

▶ "Thank You, Lord, that You never leave me."

"God has said, 'Never will I leave you; never will I forsake you.' So we say with confidence, 'The Lord is my helper; I will not be afraid. What can man do to me?'" (Hebrews 13:5–6)

▶ "Thank You, Lord, that You care for me."

"Cast all your anxiety on him because he cares for you." (1 Peter 5:7)

Because we have all been rejected, we all long to be accepted. Instead of focusing on our fear of rejection, we need to focus on reaching out to others, regardless of our differences. We respond positively when we find that others are interested in us. Think about it—when someone genuinely wants to know more about you, doesn't that warm your heart? We can be like closed rosebuds that blossom into full bloom when we meet someone who sincerely accepts us.

If you want to reach out to others, but don't know where to start, begin with ordinary questions. Your heartfelt interest will build a bridge to further communication. Ease into the questions gradually. As you talk with someone whom you don't know well, you could say, "I've never heard you talk about your childhood. Where did you grow up? What was it like living there? What was the most character-building experience of your childhood?" The Bible poetically emphasizes well-spoken words ...

**"A word aptly spoken is like apples of gold in settings of silver."
(Proverbs 25:11)**

Conversation Starters

The following questions can help you initiate conversations with others.

▶ **Questions about early family life:**

- Where were you born and raised? How did you feel about where you lived?

- What kind of work did your mom and dad do?

- What kind of relationship did you have with your father? Your mother?

- Did you have brothers and sisters? Were you emotionally close to them? Where are they now? What do they do? Are you involved in each other's lives?

- Was there an activity your family enjoyed together when you were growing up?

- What was it *really* like when you were growing up?

- If you could change anything about your childhood, what would it be?

▶ **Questions about school:**

- Did you like being a student?

- What about school did you enjoy/not enjoy?

- What do you remember most about school when you were a child?

- Did you have a favorite teacher? What made that teacher special?

- What was your favorite subject in school? Least favorite?

- What extracurricular activities did you enjoy?

- What is your most painful or embarrassing memory from your days in school?

▶ **Questions about growing up:**

- Who was your childhood hero? Why?

- What did you dream of doing when you grew up? Why?

- Did you have a best friend? Why were you so close?

- Who in your childhood encouraged you the most?

- What was the most significant event in your childhood?

- What was the most fearful time in your childhood?

- What was your first job?

- What was something you really hated doing as a child?

▶ **Questions about life today:**

- If today you could have any job in the world, what would it be?

- What do you especially enjoy doing in your free time?
- What would be your ideal vacation?
- What skill or talent do you wish you had?
- Who is investing time, concern, and energy into your life right now? How?
- What do you like most about your life today?
- If you could change anything about yourself, what would it be?

▶ **Questions about spiritual life:**

- Do you think God has a purpose for your life?
- How would you describe God?
- Did you attend a church growing up? What was it like?
- Did anything significant occur in your spiritual life when you were young?
- What is the most meaningful experience you've had in your spiritual life?
- If you could come into a true relationship with Jesus Christ, would you want to?
- What do you think God would want you to do that you haven't done yet?

Pray that you will be able to ask the right questions at the right time. When you do, you will be amazed at the difference in your relationships with others.

**"The purposes of a man's heart are deep waters, but a man of understanding draws them out."
(Proverbs 20:5)**

QUESTION: "Should I reject someone who is involved in a behavior contrary to God's Word?"

ANSWER: The Bible distinguishes between believers and nonbelievers and gives instructions as to how the local church should interact with both groups of people.

▶ Believers are not to engage in the behavior of *unbelievers* but rather are to *"come out from them and be separate"* (2 Corinthians 6:17).

▶ Believers are not to isolate themselves from nonbelievers, but rather to reach out to them just as Jesus reached out to those in sin when He lived on the earth. In fact, He was ridiculed and rebuked by the religious leaders of His day for associating with sinners and tax collectors (Matthew 9:10–12).

▶ Believers, however, are temporarily to withhold fellowship from other believers who are living *flagrantly sinful lifestyles* and to pray that this disciplinary act will bring them to repentance (1 Corinthians 5:9–13).

"But now I am writing you that you must not associate with anyone who calls himself a brother but is sexually immoral or greedy, an idolater or a slanderer, a drunkard or a swindler. With such a man do not even eat."
(1 Corinthians 5:11)

All Christians will occasionally sin and afterward repent. To reject those who show remorse and who demonstrate true repentance is unbiblical, unproductive, and unkind. Instead, we need to seek to build up a struggling believer with *compassion*, *truth*, and *encouragement*.

▶ **Compassion**

- Reach out with compassion, recognizing that everyone (including you) has sinned in various ways.

- Pray for God to give you a gentle, nonjudgmental heart as you try to bring others to restoration.

"If someone is caught in a sin, you who are spiritual should restore him gently."
(Galatians 6:1)

▶ **Truth**

- Help surface the lies that they have believed and exchange each lie with truth.

- Suggest a positive plan with practical action steps in order to break free of the habit.

"You will know the truth, and the truth will set you free." (John 8:32)

▶ Encouragement

- Affirm their God-given worth as they choose to live in the strength of Christ.
- Praise them when they make small steps toward Christlike behavior.

"Encourage one another and build each other up, just as in fact you are doing." (1 Thessalonians 5:11)

If we engage in anything that grieves the heart of God, someone could rightly reject us. If a relationship is forbidden by God (such as adultery), ending that relationship is the right thing to do. Any attempt to continue the relationship needs to be rejected. If you are experiencing the piercing pain of having been rejected only because that relationship was not right in God's sight, you can still hope for a bright tomorrow despite your despair today. God sees your hurt and feels compassion for you, even if your painful circumstances are a result of your own bad choices. Learning from your mistakes and allowing God to change your life is still possible. God has always been in the business of rescuing people from the grip of sinful behavioral patterns and turning their lives into blessings.

▶ Acknowledge to God the sinful behavior that led to your being rejected.

"If we confess our sins, he is faithful and just and will forgive us our sins and purify us from all unrighteousness." (1 John 1:9)

▶ Ask God to bring you to the point of seeing your sin as He sees it.

"Search me, O God, and know my heart; test me and know my anxious thoughts. See if there is any offensive way in me, and lead me in the way everlasting." (Psalm 139:23–24)

▶ Agree with God that your behavior was egregious to Him and deserving of His disapproval and discipline.

"For I know my transgressions, and my sin is always before me. Against you, you only, have I sinned and done what is evil in your sight, so that you are proved right when you speak and justified when you judge." (Psalm 51:3–4)

▶ Assume the responsibility of asking forgiveness from the person(s) you have offended.

"If you are offering your gift at the altar and there remember that your brother has something against you, leave your gift there in front of the altar. First go and be reconciled to your brother; then come and offer your gift." (Matthew 5:23–24)

▶ Ascertain what need you were seeking to have met through your behavior.

"Surely you desire truth in the inner parts; you teach me wisdom in the inmost place." (Psalm 51:6)

▶ Align your thinking with God's thinking by engaging in daily Bible reading and Scripture meditation and memorization.

"I have hidden your word in my heart that I might not sin against you." (Psalm 119:11)

▶ Apply the truths of God's Word to your life.

"Show me your ways, O LORD, teach me your paths; guide me in your truth and teach me, for you are God my Savior, and my hope is in you all day long." (Psalm 25:4–5)

▶ Act out of your identity in Christ.

"I have been crucified with Christ and I no longer live, but Christ lives in me. The life I live in the body, I live by faith in the Son of God, who loved me and gave himself for me." (Galatians 2:20)

▶ Associate with others who are seeking to live lives that are pleasing to God.

"Blessed is the man who does not walk in the counsel of the wicked or stand in the way of sinners or sit in the seat of mockers. But his delight is in the law of the LORD, and on his law he meditates day and night." (Psalm 1:1–2)

Some people present a wrong picture of what it means to become a Christian—"Come to Christ and all your problems are solved." Jesus never suggested such! In fact, the Bible makes it crystal clear that we are *called to suffer.* Clearly, Jesus suffered very real rejection by the religious leaders of His day. But He was also rejected by dear friends and family, yet He was not emotionally devastated, neither was he derailed from His mission. Why? He knew the secret of being an overcomer: He *"entrusted himself to him who judges justly."* Jesus entrusted His very being into the hands of His heavenly Father, whom He knew would judge justly. When you experience rejection, you too will be an overcomer by following in the footsteps of Jesus.

"If you suffer for doing good and you endure it, this is commendable before God. To this you were called, because Christ suffered for you, leaving you an example, that you should follow in his steps. ... When they hurled their insults at him, he did not retaliate; when he suffered, he made no threats. Instead, he entrusted himself to him who judges justly." (1 Peter 2:20–21, 23)

▶ **Jesus knew to expect unjust hatred.**

And He tells you to expect unjust hatred.

"They hated me without reason."
(John 15:25)

"I have chosen you out of the world. That is why the world hates you." (John 15:19)

▶ **Jesus knew to expect persecution.**

And He tells you to expect persecution.

"Blessed are those who are persecuted because of righteousness, for theirs is the kingdom of heaven." (Matthew 5:10)

"If they persecuted me, they will persecute you also." (John 15:20)

▶ **Jesus had enemies, yet He loved them.**

And He tells you to love your enemies and do good to them.

"Love your enemies." (Matthew 5:44)

"Love your enemies, do good to them."
(Luke 6:35)

▶ **Jesus prayed for those who persecuted Him.**

And He says to pray for your persecutors.

"Father, forgive them, for they do not know what they are doing." (Luke 23:34)

"Pray for those who persecute you."
(Matthew 5:44)

▶ **Jesus modeled forgiveness toward those who sinned against Him.**

And He says to forgive those who sin against you.

"Forgive, and you will be forgiven."
(Luke 6:37)

"If you forgive men when they sin against you, your heavenly Father will also forgive you." (Matthew 6:14)

▶ **Jesus understood that those rejecting Him were really rejecting His Father.**

And He says that those rejecting you are really rejecting Him.

"He who rejects me rejects him who sent me."
(Luke 10:16)

"He who rejects you rejects me."
(Luke 10:16)

▶ **Jesus, when rejected, was dependent on His Father for every word He spoke.**

And He says, when you are rejected, be dependent on the Holy Spirit for every word you speak.

"There is a judge for the one who rejects me and does not accept my words; that very word which I spoke will condemn him at the last day. For I did not speak of my own accord, but the Father who sent me commanded me what to say and how to say it." (John 12:48–49)

"Whenever you are arrested and brought to trial, do not worry beforehand about what to say. Just say whatever is given you at the time, for it is not you speaking, but the Holy Spirit." (Mark 13:11)

▶**Jesus knew that some in Jerusalem had killed and stoned prophets and now Herod wanted to kill Him (Luke 13:31), but love—not fear—was Jesus' focus.**

And He says though some want to kill you, don't let fear of people be your focus.

"You who kill the prophets and stone those sent to you, how often I have longed to gather your children together, as a hen gathers her chicks under her wings, but you were not willing!" (Luke 13:34)

"Do not be afraid of those who kill the body but cannot kill the soul. Rather, be afraid of the One who can destroy both soul and body in hell." (Matthew 10:28)

▶ **Jesus said He would be rejected, but in the end there would be blessing.**

And He said you will be rejected, but in the end there will be blessing.

"He then began to teach them that the Son of Man must suffer many things and be rejected by the elders, chief priests and teachers of the law, and that he must be killed and after three days rise again." (Mark 8:31)

"Blessed are you when men hate you, when they exclude you and insult you and reject your name as evil, because of the Son of Man." (Luke 6:22)

▶ **Jesus expected trouble as He submitted to the Father's purpose—yet Jesus was an overcomer!**

And He says for you to expect trouble, but when trouble comes, if you will submit to the Father's purpose you'll be an overcomer!

"Now my heart is troubled, and what shall I say? 'Father, save me from this hour'? No, it was for this very reason I came to this hour." (John 12:27)

"In this world you will have trouble. But take heart! I have overcome the world." (John 16:33)

MY PRAYER OF RESPONSE TO REJECTION

*"My Lord Jesus,
I will live with Your hope—
even when life looks hopeless.*

*I will not harbor hate—
even when I'm ignored.*

*I will live with Your peace—
even when I'm rejected.*

*I will love with Your love—
even when I am scorned.*

*I will pray with Your heart—
even for those who hurt me.*

*I'll forgive with Your grace—
even when I'm betrayed.*

*I won't focus on fear—
for I know You are faithful.*

*I won't let heartache reign—
I'll move forward with faith!*

Your humble child, Amen."

SCRIPTURES TO MEMORIZE

What will **God** do when I have **fear** or become **dismayed**?

> "*Do not **fear**, for I am with you; do not be **dismayed**, for I am your **God**. I will strengthen you and help you; I will uphold you with my righteous right hand.*" (Isaiah 41:10)

Why **will the Lord not reject you**?

> "*For the sake of his great name **the LORD will not reject his people**, because the LORD was pleased to make you his own.*" (1 Samuel 12:22)

How does **the Lord** respond to those who are **brokenhearted and crushed in spirit**?

> "*The LORD is close to the **brokenhearted and** saves those who are **crushed in spirit**.*" (Psalm 34:18)

What will **never fail because of the Lord's great love** for us?

> "*Because of the LORD's great love we are not consumed, for his compassions **never fail**.*" (Lamentations 3:22)

How can I know that when others **reject me**, they are actually rejecting Christ?

*"He who listens to you listens to me; he who rejects you **rejects me**; but he who **rejects me** rejects him who sent me."* (Luke 10:16)

Why should I **not be afraid** or **discouraged**?

*"The LORD himself goes before you and will be with you; he will never leave you nor forsake you. Do **not be afraid**; do not be **discouraged**."* (Deuteronomy 31:8)

Even when you are **forsaken** by your **father and mother**, who will never reject you?

*"Though my **father and mother forsake** me, the LORD will receive me."* (Psalm 27:10)

Why are we **called children of God**?

*"How great is the love the Father has lavished on us, that we should be **called children of God**! And that is what we are!"* (1 John 3:1)

How should you respond to **God, who has not rejected** you or **withheld His love** from you?

*"Praise be to **God, who has not rejected** my prayer or **withheld his love** from me!"* (Psalm 66:20)

Can you name at least five things that will never **separate us from the love of God**?

> *"I am convinced that neither death nor life, neither angels nor demons, neither the present nor the future, nor any powers, neither height nor depth, nor anything else in all creation, will be able to **separate us from the love of God** that is in Christ Jesus our Lord."* (Romans 8:38–39)

NOTES

1. Adapted from *Merriam-Webster Collegiate Dictionary,* s.v. "Rejection," http://www.m-w.com (2001).

2. James Strong, *Strong's Greek Lexicon,* electronic ed., Online Bible Millennium Ed. v. 1.13 (Timnathserah Inc., July 6, 2002).

3. Adapted from *Merriam-Webster Collegiate Dictionary,* s.v. "Reject."

4. Strong, *Strong's Greek Lexicon.*

5. Adapted from *Merriam-Webster Collegiate Dictionary,* s.v. "Reject."

6. James Strong, *Strong's Hebrew Lexicon,* electronic ed., Online Bible Millennium Ed. v. 1.13 (Timnathserah Inc., July 6, 2002).

7. Adapted from *Merriam-Webster Collegiate Dictionary,* s.v. "Accept."

8. Strong, *Strong's Greek Lexicon.*

9. Robert S. McGee, *The Search for Significance: Book and Workbook,* Revised (Houston, TX: Rapha, 1987), 219-20.

10. McGee, *The Search for Significance,* 54-60.

11. McGee, *The Search for Significance,* 54-55.

12. Charles Solomon, *The Ins and Out of Rejection* (Littleton, CO: Heritage House, 1976), 42-47.

13. Solomon, *The Ins and Out of Rejection*, 47-54.

14. Adapted from Jeff VanVonderen, *Tired of Trying to Measure Up* (Minneapolis, MN: Bethany House, 1989), 75.

15. Solomon, *The Ins and Out of Rejection*, 49-50.

16. Solomon, *The Ins and Out of Rejection*, 13-18.

17. Solomon, *The Ins and Out of Rejection*, 18-25, 40-42; Charles Solomon, *The Rejection Syndrome* (Wheaton, IL: Tyndale House, 1982), 29-52.

18. This chart adapted from McGee, *The Search for Significance*, 135.

19. McGee, *The Search for Significance*, 136.

20. McGee, *The Search for Significance*, 13.

21. Marshall Bryant Hodge, *Your Fear of Love* (Garden City, NY: Doubleday, 1967), 26.

22. McGee, *The Search for Significance*, 137-53.

SELECTED BIBLIOGRAPHY

Hodge, Marshall Bryant. *Your Fear of Love.* Garden City, NY: Doubleday, 1967.

Hunt, June. *Counseling Through Your Bible Handbook.* Eugene, Oregon: Harvest House Publishers, 2007.

Hunt, June. *How to Forgive... When You Don't Feel Like It.* Eugene, Oregon: Harvest House Publishers, 2007.

Hunt, June. *How to Handle Your Emotions.* Eugene, Oregon: Harvest House Publishers, 2008.

Hunt, June. *Seeing Yourself Through God's Eyes.* Eugene, Oregon: Harvest House Publishers, 2008.

McGee, Robert S. *The Search for Significance.* 2d ed. Houston, TX: Rapha, 1990.

Solomon, Charles. *The Ins and Out of Rejection.* Littleton, CO: Heritage House, 1976.

Solomon, Charles. *The Rejection Syndrome.* Wheaton, IL: Tyndale House, 1982.

VanVonderen, Jeff. *Tired of Trying to Measure Up.* Minneapolis, MN: Bethany House, 1989.

Wright, H. Norman. *Real Solutions for Overcoming Discouragement, Rejection, and the Blues.* Ann Arbor, MI: Vine, 2001.

June Hunt's HOPE FOR THE HEART minibooks are biblically-based, and full of practical advice that is relevant, spiritually-fulfilling and wholesome.

HOPE FOR THE HEART TITLES

Adultery .... ISBN 9781596366848
Alcohol & Drug Abuse .... ISBN 9781596366596
Anger .... ISBN 9781596366411
Codependency .... ISBN 9781596366510
Conflict Resolution .... ISBN 9781596366473
Confrontation .... ISBN 9781596366886
Considering Marriage .... ISBN 9781596366763
Decision Making .... ISBN 9781596366534
Depression .... ISBN 9781596366497
Domestic Violence .... ISBN 9781596366824
Fear .... ISBN 9781596366701
Forgiveness .... ISBN 9781596366435
Friendship .... ISBN 9781596368828
Gambling .... ISBN 9781596366862
Grief .... ISBN 9781596366572
Guilt .... ISBN 9781596366961
Hope .... ISBN 9781596366558
Loneliness .... ISBN 9781596366909
Manipulation .... ISBN 9781596366749
Marriage .... ISBN 9781596368941
Parenting .... ISBN 9781596366725
Reconciliation .... ISBN 9781596368897
Rejection .... ISBN 9781596366787
Self-Worth .... ISBN 9781596366688
Sexual Integrity .... ISBN 9781596366947
Singleness .... ISBN 9781596368774
Stress .... ISBN 9781596368996
Success Through Failure .... ISBN 9781596366923
Suicide Prevention .... ISBN 9781596366800
Verbal & Emotional Abuse .... ISBN 9781596366459

www.aspirepress.com